Discovering
SLUGS AND SNAILS

Jennifer Coldrey

The Bookwright Press
New York · 1987

Discovering Nature

Discovering Ants
Discovering Bees and Wasps
Discovering Beetles
Discovering Birds of Prey
Discovering Butterflies and Moths
Discovering Crabs and Lobsters
Discovering Crickets and Grasshoppers
Discovering Ducks, Geese and Swans
Discovering Flies

Discovering Flowering Plants
Discovering Frogs and Toads
Discovering Rabbits and Hares
Discovering Rats and Mice
Discovering Seabirds
Discovering Slugs and Snails
Discovering Snakes and Lizards
Discovering Spiders
Discovering Squirrels
Discovering Worms

Further titles are in preparation

First published in the
United States in 1987 by
The Bookwright Press
387 Park Avenue South
New York, NY 10016

First published in 1987 by
Wayland (Publishers) Limited
61 Western Road, Hove
East Sussex BN3 1JD, England

ISBN 0-531-18128-6

Library of Congress Catalog Card Number: 86-72824

Typeset by DP Press Ltd., Sevenoaks, Kent
Printed in Italy by Sagdos S.p.A., Milan

Editor: Joan Walters

Cover   *Roman snails, large, edible land snails, live in chalky areas of the British countryside.*

Frontispiece   *This dragon-like creature is a sea slug found on the Great Barrier Reef of Australia.*

Contents

1
Introducing Slugs and Snails

The giant triton, one of the largest sea snails, can grow to 40 cm (15.6 in) long.

Slugs and snails are closely related to each other. They belong to a large group of soft-bodied animals called **mollusks**, which includes many so-called "shellfish" and animals such as octopus and squid. Like other mollusks, slugs and snails have no bones. Their soft, slippery skin is often covered by a shell, but their bodies dry out very easily because their skin is not waterproof. For this reason, most slugs and snails live in damp or wet places; they also produce a lot of slime which helps to keep their skin moist.

There are well over 70,000 different kinds of slugs and snails in the world. They are found in all kinds of places, including gardens, woods, fields, cliffs and marshes. Some live in freshwater ponds, lakes and rivers, while many more live in the sea.

Most slugs and snails cannot survive in very cold or very hot, dry places – those living on land prefer warm, moist climates and many live in the **tropics**. However, there are snails that survive in the desert, and others that live in thermal springs as hot as 44°C (111.2°F). Some of the smallest snails are no bigger than a pinhead. There are tiny sea slugs too, just a few millimeters long, that live among the sand grains on the shore.

At the other extreme, the largest land snail is a giant African snail with a shell about 20 cm (8 in) long and 10 cm (4 in) in diameter. But the largest slugs and snails are found in the sea.

The largest sea slugs are called sea hares. This particular kind grow as long as 20 cm (8 in) but there are others that reach 40 cm (15.6 in) and weigh up to 7 kilos (15½ lb).

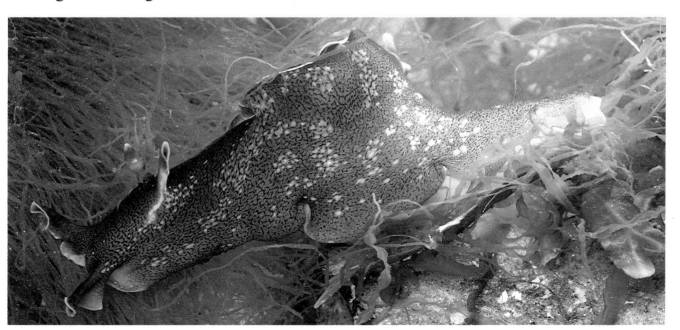

2
What Slugs and Snails are Like

You can see this banded snail's small, black eyes on the end of its tentacles. If touched, land slugs and snails pull their eyes inside their hollow tentacles, like the pushed in fingers of a rubber glove.

The Bodies of Slugs and Snails

Slugs and snails make up a group of mollusks called **gastropods**. This name comes from two Greek words, "gaster" meaning belly and "pes, podos" meaning a foot. This describes how slugs and snails move around, as though on the belly, but in fact on a large soft, muscular part of the body called the foot. Joined to the foot, at the front end of the body, is the head. The rest of the body is carried in a lump on the back of the animal. Covering this lump is a thin cloak of skin called the **mantle**. A snail's mantle is not easy to see since it is largely covered by the shell.

Between the mantle and the main body is a space called the mantle cavity. This is much larger in some slugs and snails than in others, while in some it may be absent altogether. Slugs and snails take in water or air

A slug can stretch its body out to make it long and thin or bunch it up into a fat lump!

for breathing through the mantle cavity. Waste material is passed out through it too.

The head of a slug or snail carries one or two pairs of tentacles, a pair of eyes and a mouth. The mouth has a long, tongue-like structure called the **radula**, which bears rows of tiny teeth. The size, shape and number of teeth are different in every type of animal. Slugs and snails can slide the radula back and forth so that the teeth act like a file or grater, rasping at their food and carrying it back into the mouth like a conveyor belt. Some slugs and snails can pierce and even poison prey with their radulae.

A close-up of a pond snail's mouth showing the tongue-like radula, covered with teeth.

A snail climbing on a pane of glass. The stripes across its body are bands of muscle.

Movement and Senses

Slugs and snails are slow-moving animals. They use the broad sole of the foot to crawl along and they glide on a layer of special slimy **mucus**, which they produce from **glands** in the foot. The sole of the foot is also covered with many tiny, hair-like structures called **cilia**. In some smaller snails these beat rhythmically and help to propel the animal along.

Most slugs and snails move forward by alternately contracting and expanding bands of muscles in the foot. This causes waves of movement to sweep along the foot and push the animal forward. The layer of slime allows a slug or snail to move over rough or sharp surfaces without damaging its body. The slime is also sticky, which explains why slugs and snails are able to climb up or down, and even cling upside down to many surfaces, even glass.

As a slug or snail moves forward, it senses out its surroundings with its eyes and tentacles. The eyes cannot see very clearly, but they can tell whether it is light or dark and can probably see dim shapes. The smaller

A banded snail stretches out its body as it moves along a log.

As a slug or snail moves, it leaves behind a sticky trail of slime that allows it to climb up and down. This is a black slug.

tentacles on the head are used for smelling and feeling. Other parts of the body, including much of the skin, are also sensitive to touch. Some sea slugs and snails have small tentacles around the edge of the foot or mantle, which they use to feel and even "taste" their surroundings.

More About Snails

Snails are gastropods with an obvious shell that is made of a chalky substance and is produced by the snail from the edge of its mantle. It is covered by a thin horny, outer layer, which gives the shell its glossy shine.

The shell forms a hard, protective case into which the snail can pull its whole body for safety. Many underwater

This is a common whelk, a kind of snail that lives in the ocean. You can see its operculum (a round plate of shell) under the middle part of the main shell.

snails carry another small, round plate of shell, called the **operculum**, on the foot. This seals the mouth of the shell like a door when the animal retreats inside.

The shells of all gastropod snails are formed in one piece. They are usually spirally coiled in a clockwise direction, although a few types do coil the opposite way. As a snail grows bigger, it adds further coils to the shell and the upper parts of its body become twisted. The body is attached to the shell by a strong muscle, which is fixed to a central column within the spiral. Some snails, such as limpets and abalones, are only coiled in the young stages; they become less twisted as they grow and the adult shells are uncoiled.

Some snail shells are coiled into tall spires or cones, others form round, flat spirals, while limpet shells are uncoiled and tent-like in shape. Many

This European cowrie, like many sea snails, has a snorkel-like extension of the mantle, which sucks in clean water for breathing.

snail shells are banded with lines or spots of color; some are smooth and glossy, others rough and ridged. Many sea snail shells are very large and heavy, with knobs or spines sticking out from the surface.

More About Slugs

Slugs are simply snails without shells. At least, they have no obvious shell, but traces of a shell are usually present inside the body, hidden within the mantle; some land slugs even have a tiny piece of shell on the outside of their bodies. The mantle of land slugs forms a fleshy saddle over the back of the animal. The mantle of many sea slugs is drawn out into lobes or flaps that stick out from the sides.

Like snails, slugs can stretch out their bodies or shrink them up into a small lump by contracting their muscles. Slugs' bodies are not coiled or twisted inside a shell, which means that they can stretch out and squeeze into narrow cracks and crevices to shelter. Although they have no hard outer shell, slugs are protected from drying out, and from other damage, by being covered with a thick layer of

A great gray slug glides up a twig. Slugs are usually longer, flatter and more streamlined than snails.

mucus, which they produce from glands all over their bodies. Their skins are often tough, while many sea slugs have small spiky pieces of limestone embedded in their backs.

Land slugs are usually dull in color – black, brown, white, yellowish or gray, while many have spots or patterns on the skin. Some have smooth skins; others have rough skins, with deep ridges and furrows, and sometimes warts, on their backs.

A spotted sea slug from Australia's Great Barrier Reef. It has two tentacles at its head end and a ring of gills at its rear.

Sea slugs are often very beautiful and brightly colored. Many have strange, elaborate shapes, some with tentacle-like projections sticking out in rows or bunches from their backs. These may be used as **gills** for breathing, or they may be sensitive to touch.

3
Where Slugs and Snails Live

A Roman snail hibernating. Once sealed up snails can sleep, without feeding, for several months until better weather returns.

On Land

Land slugs and snails are often hard to find. During the day most of them hide away in damp, shady places – under stones, logs or rotting leaves, among plants or deep in the soil. They are active mainly at night, but sometimes come out on cool, wet days when there is no danger of their bodies drying out in the sun. Most snails live in places where there is plenty of chalk or limestone in the rocks and soil. They need chalk to help build their shells. Slugs, on the other hand, are not so dependent on limestone and can live in a wider variety of **habitats**.

If the weather becomes extremely hot and dry, most snails withdraw inside their shells and go to sleep. This is called **aestivation**. They seal the shell opening with a thick layer of mucus which then hardens to form a waterproof plug. In very cold weather, slugs and snails do exactly the same – they go to sleep, or hibernate, until warmer weather returns. Slugs creep underground or into rock crevices; snails often gather in groups in a sheltered place, where they seal up their shells to protect their bodies from the cold.

Most land slugs and snails breathe through a hole in the mantle on the right side of the body. The hole leads into the front of the mantle cavity, which acts like a lung. Like our lungs, the lining of the mantle cavity is thin, moist and well supplied with blood vessels to absorb oxygen from the air.

The breathing hole in the side of this netted slug opens and closes rhythmically.

In Fresh Water

Freshwater snails live in ponds, lakes, rivers and streams all over the world. Some like shallow water or marshy ground; others survive on the bottom of deep lakes. Slugs do not live in fresh water.

Freshwater snails move around by crawling over stones or mud on the bottom, by climbing on plants, or by clinging upside down to the surface of the water. They are active most of the time, unless the water freezes or becomes extremely cold. Although there is little danger they will dry up, water snails tend to hide away from bright sunshine.

Freshwater limpets, like this, are found clinging to stones or plants in lakes and fast-flowing streams all over the world.

Most freshwater snails have only one pair of tentacles, which they cannot withdraw. Their eyes are at the base of these tentacles.

The ramshorn snail has a flattened spiral shell. It can live in stagnant water where there is very little oxygen.

Although they live underwater, many pond snails breathe air from the atmosphere. They have a lung, as land snails do, and they come to the surface every now and then to take in a gulp of air. Pond snails can also absorb oxygen from the water into their bodies – either through the mantle cavity, or sometimes through their skin. Some deep-water snails can, in fact, breathe without ever having to come to the surface for air. Other freshwater snails have gills inside the mantle cavity that absorb oxygen for breathing. They live mainly in rivers and streams where there is plenty of dissolved oxygen in the fast-flowing water.

In the Sea – Crawlers and Creepers

Edible periwinkles and a limpet cling to the rocks at low tide.

The sea contains an enormous number of different kinds of slugs and snails. They are very different from land gastropods. Many live in shallow water around the coasts, where they crawl along or cling to rocks, seaweed or coral; others burrow below the sand or mud and some live on the bottom of the sea in deeper waters.

A rocky shore is a good place to look for sea slugs and snails. Those that live on the upper shore or between the tides, have to spend long periods of time out of the water. To avoid drying out, limpets clamp themselves firmly onto the rocks, using the muscular foot like a suction pad. Their strong grip and broad, heavy shells prevent them from being swept away or damaged by the buffeting waves. Sea slugs and other sea snails, such as periwinkles, whelks and topshells, shelter in rock crevices or under seaweed. Snails use the horny operculum on the end of their foot to close their shell openings.

Most bottom-dwelling slugs and snails creep or glide across the seabed, using their foot in the usual way. Burrowing snails, such as the moonshell or necklace shells, have an especially broad front end to the foot that they use, like a bulldozer blade, to push themselves into the sand. The conchs crawl slowly across the seabed, using a long, claw-like operculum to dig into the sand and haul themselves along.

Nearly all sea slugs and snails breathe through gills, although there are some that can absorb oxygen through the entire surface of the body. The gills of most sea snails are inside the mantle cavity.

Many sea slugs have no mantle cavity and the gills often stick out from the sides or back of the body.

The sea slug, Glaucus, *is about 3 cm (1.17 in) long. It lives at the surface of the water. It does not swim, but floats upside down, buoyed up by a bubble of air in its stomach.*

In the Sea – Swimmers and Floaters

Although most sea slugs and snails are bottom-dwellers, there are some that occasionally swim or float in the open sea. Sea slugs, with their soft, flexible bodies, are especially suited to swimming. Many can move through the water by flexing the muscles of their body in a wave-like movement. The foot or mantle is often extended on either side of the body into wide folds. The sea slugs use these, like paddles, to propel themselves along. Sea hares can swim in this way, although they also spend a lot of time crawling along the bottom.

A few sea slugs and snails spend their entire lives afloat among the **plankton** in the sea. Sea butterflies have two wing-like flaps at the front end of their bodies, which they use like oars for swimming. Other gastropods swim upside down near the surface, with the large foot spread out sideways, like a fin. Their bodies are almost transparent and this helps to protect them from hungry fish and other **predators**.

The violet or bubble-raft sea snail actually floats right at the surface of the ocean. It hangs upside down, supported by a raft of bubbles, which it traps into a floating mass of mucus. It spends its whole life drifting at the surface, feeding mainly on sea jellies which it bumps into by chance.

Above   *These swimming gastropods, called sea butterflies, are often found among the plankton in northern waters.*

Left   *The lovely bubble-raft snail floats at the surface of the ocean. Its shell is about 2 cm (0.78 in) across.*

4
Food and Feeding

Slugs and snails often eat fungi. This slug is eating a kind of toadstool called the fly agaric, which is poisonous to humans.

Plant-eaters, Scavengers and Filter-feeders

Most land slugs and snails are **herbivorous**. They feed on plants, eating leaves, shoots, roots, flowers, fruits and fungi, but they especially like dead and rotting vegetation. Some feed or **scavenge** on dead animals too. Land slugs and snails have strong jaws and broad radulae covered with thousands of tiny teeth which they use to cut, grind and shred their food. Many rasp away at rocks and soil from which they obtain useful minerals, including chalk.

Freshwater snails are largely herbivorous too. They browse on the tiny **algae** and other microscopic creatures that grow on the surface of waterweeds and stones. They eat decaying plants too, while some, including the great pond snail, scavenge on small dead fish.

A garden snail grazing on lichen.

Several underwater snails and slugs feed on tiny food particles floating in the water or lying in the mud or sand on the bottom. Some catch their food by pushing out threads or nets of mucus that trap the particles and then pull them back into the mouth. Others filter the food through extra-large comb-like gills as they draw water in and out of the mantle cavity.

Many sea snails are plant-eaters. Certain periwinkles and other shore snails feed on larger seaweeds, while limpets, topshells and others living higher on the shore, eat **lichens** and algae growing on the rocks. Among the plant-eating sea slugs are the sea hares, which feed on large seaweeds. Another group of very small sea slugs feed by piercing into seaweeds with their one row of spear-like teeth, and sucking out the juices.

The pelican's foot snail (a sea snail) uses its long proboscis to probe in muddy gravel for tiny particles of food.

Carnivorous Slugs and Snails

One or two land slugs and snails eat living animals, including insects, earthworms and other slugs and snails. But most **carnivorous** slugs and snails live in the sea. For many, finding food is an easy matter – they simply crawl slowly over their **prey**.

This common gray sea slug is eating a beadlet anemone.

The animals they eat are fixed to the seabed, often living in colonies, and they include sponges, sea-squirts, sea-anemones, corals, moss animals and fish eggs.

Other carnivorous sea slugs and snails are more active in their search for food. Some of the swimming sea slugs attack tiny fish and shrimp-like animals; others feed on small sea jellies and on other small gastropods that float in the plankton.

Many carnivorous sea snails (and some sea slugs) have the mouth at the end of a long, snout-like **proboscis**, which they push out and use for probing into their prey. The teeth on their radulae, although often few in number, are sharp and curved for cutting and seizing flesh. Many sea snails feed on other shelled mollusks, such as cockles and mussels, and some burrow into the sand to reach their prey. Several first attack the

victim by smothering it with the foot. Large whelks grip their prey, such as clams or oysters, with the foot; the whelk then wedges open the **bivalve** shell with the lip of its own shell, before starting to eat the soft parts inside.

Other sea snails, such as dog whelks and oysterdrills, bore a hole

Some large sea snails feed on sea urchins or starfish. Here, the giant triton, or trumpet shell, of Australia is feeding on the famous crown of thorns starfish that can seriously damage coral reefs.

through the shell of the victim with the radula. Some release a special chemical to help soften the shell.

5
Reproduction

Giant leopard slugs mating in midair, suspended on a rope of slimy mucus.

Mating on Land

Most land slugs and snails are **hermaphrodite**. This means that every animal is both male and female and able to produce both eggs and **sperm**. When two animals mate they exchange sperm with each other and so **fertilize** each other's eggs.

Many land snails mate at night when it is cool and dark. They first perform a courtship dance, circling each other and caressing each other with their tentacles. As they draw closer they raise the fronts of their bodies and press the "soles" of each foot together. Each snail then shoots a sharp chalky **spicule**, like a dart about 5 mm (0.2 in) long, into the other's body. This stimulates them to produce sperm, which is passed through the **penis** into the female opening of the partner. The sexual openings are at the front of the body.

After clinging together for several hours, the two snails move apart. Each stores the sperm inside its body until the eggs are ready to be laid. The eggs are fertilized just before laying. Land slugs mate in a similar way, wrapping their bodies together in a mass of slime. Some carry out their courtship in midair, suspended from a branch or wall on a rope of mucus.

Land slugs and snails usually lay

Two garden snails mating. After shooting out their chalky "darts," they exchange sperm and so fertilize each other's eggs.

their eggs a week or two after mating, although in cold weather, they may not lay them for several months. Instead of laying eggs, some land snails keep their eggs inside the body to develop, later giving birth to fully formed young snails.

Mating Under Water

Many pond snails are hermaphrodites, and mate the way land snails do. Other freshwater snails, and nearly all sea snails, have separate male and female animals. The male usually has a penis with which he injects sperm into the female through her sexual opening. The female's eggs are usually fertilized inside her body; but in limpets, topshells and abalones, fertilization takes place outside the body. The males release a cloud of milky sperm into the water at the same time as nearby females shed their eggs into the sea. Sperm and eggs then join together and from the fertilized eggs, young snails immediately start to form.

Before mating, these sea hares perform a courtship dance. Courtship is a special kind of behavior that attracts a mate.

Male and female Antarctic limpets releasing their sperm and eggs into the water where fertilization takes place.

A stack of slipper limpets. The oldest, at the bottom, are females, the middle ones hermaphrodites, and the upper ones males.

It is hard to tell whether some sea snails are male or female, because they change sex as they grow older. Slipper limpets, for example, start off life as males, later become both male and female and finally end up as females. Slipper limpets usually live, one on top of the other, in chains; the oldest, at the bottom, are females, the youngest, at the top, are males.

All sea slugs are hermaphrodites, acting as both male and female, and mate the way land slugs do. Sea hares, however, frequently mate in chains, so that each animal acts as a male to the animal in front, but female to the animal behind. Many sea slugs and snails, even those living in deeper water, come inshore to breed and lay their eggs in shallow water.

Eggs and Young

Most land slugs and snails lay their eggs in the soil or under rotting leaves, logs or stones. Garden snails lay between 20 to 50 eggs at a time; others lay fewer, while some lay well over a hundred. Depending on the weather, it may take several weeks, or perhaps months for the young to hatch. They emerge as miniature slugs or snails, exactly like their parents, although often a different color from the adults. After eating the remains of their eggshells, they start to work their way above ground and then to feed on plants or soil.

Freshwater snails, and many sea slugs and snails, lay their eggs in a mass of jelly, which they stick to stones, plants or to any other surface they can find. Other marine slugs and snails deposit their eggs in long strings or ribbons of mucus, which

The garden snail lays large, yolky eggs. Snails' eggs are usually round, pearly white and encased in tough shells.

they sometimes coil or fold around weeds or rocks. Dog whelks, some periwinkles and various other sea snails produce their eggs in tough, horny capsules, which they attach to the seabed, either singly, or in grape-like clusters. Although there may be many eggs inside each capsule, usually only a few hatch, these youngsters having eaten the others.

Most baby sea slugs and snails (and also some freshwater snails) hatch

Newly hatched land snails have fragile, transparent shells with only two whorls. Adult snail shells have four or five whorls.

out, not as tiny adults, but as free-swimming **larvae** that look quite unlike their parents. After drifting in the sea for many days (or sometimes weeks), and providing they are not eaten, the tiny larvae settle on the bottom where they grow into young slugs or snails.

6
Enemies and Survival

The song thrush has a special way of breaking into a snail's shell to get at the flesh. It holds the snail in its beak and hammers it down on a stone.

Enemies on Land

Slugs and snails have many enemies on land. Snails are especially at risk. They are eaten by various birds, including crows, starlings and thrushes.

Slugs are not so easy to eat. They are covered with a very sticky slime that many birds and other predators find unpleasant. However, some slugs and many snails are eaten by hedgehogs, badgers, shrews, moles, mice, frogs and toads. Many of these predators hunt at night, which is the time when slugs and snails are most active.

Slugs and snails are also attacked by smaller animals, including centipedes, certain beetles and carnivorous slugs and snails. These predators also eat the eggs and young. Many snails are killed by **parasitic** flies that lay their eggs in the snail's

The larva of the glow-worm beetle eats nothing but snails. It crawls into the shell and devours the soft flesh inside.

themselves by spurting out jets of milky mucus at the attacker. Slugs can also escape by crawling into narrow cracks and crevices. Snails try to escape by withdrawing deep into their shells and closing up the opening with a plug of slime (or an operculum if they have one). Many have shells that are the same color or pattern as their background, making it difficult for enemies to spot them.

body, or in its eggs, where the grubs hatch out and start to eat their **host**.

Most slugs are protected from being eaten because of the slippery and bad-tasting slime that covers their bodies — some large land slugs actually defend

An Australian blue-tongued lizard eating a snail.

Underwater Enemies

Fish are among the chief enemies of slugs and snails living underwater. Freshwater snails are also eaten by ducks and by wading birds such as

A shore crab eating a periwinkle. Many sea snails are eaten by crabs.

herons, while frogs, turtles and otters often feed on them too. Carnivorous diving beetles and their larvae also prey on freshwater snails.

Sea slugs and snails have other enemies. Those living close to the shore may be eaten by sea birds, as well as by fish, crabs and other carnivorous sea snails. The free-floating sea slugs and snails (which include many larvae) are preyed upon by fish and jellyfish, or they may be scooped up into the huge mouths of plankton-feeding whales. Many bottom-living sea snails are attacked by starfish which cling to the snail's shell with their sucker-like feet. Cowries and moonshells can protect themselves from starfish by wrapping large flaps of the foot or mantle over their shells, so that the starfish's feet cannot get a grip on them.

Most sea snails can protect themselves from attack by withdrawing into their shells and sealing up the entrance with the operculum. Periwinkles hide away in cracks and crevices, while limpets and abalones clamp themselves firmly to the rocks so that it is not easy to pry them off.

Many sea slugs are protected from predators because their coloring hides them perfectly against the background over which they crawl. Others display vivid colors, which warn predators that they are poisonous or taste unpleasant.

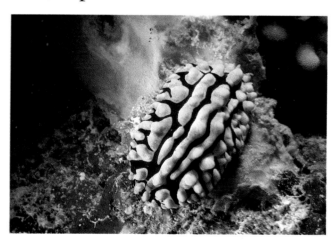

This colorful sea slug is poisonous to fish and other animals that try to eat it. Predators soon learn to leave it alone.

Humans as Enemies

Humans harm slugs and snails in various ways. Unfortunately, some land slugs and snails do serious damage to our crops. Many people kill them by putting down poisonous slug pellets, or by spraying the plants with **pesticides**.

Some sea snails are a pest on commercial shellfish beds, because they damage mussels, oysters and clams, which people like to eat. Slipper limpets often live on top of oysters or mussels, competing with them for food and often smothering them. Whelks, oysterdrills and sting winkles are predatory sea snails that kill oysters, mussels and other bivalves, by drilling holes into their shells and eating the contents. Shellfish farmers try to control these pests by continually removing the snails and their eggs.

In many parts of the world, people enjoy eating snails. In France, various land snails are cultivated on special snail farms. In Britain and the Mediterranean, people collect edible periwinkles from the shore to eat, while in other parts of the world, the large, fleshy foot of the abalone is a favorite food.

A slipper limpet on top of a common mussel. Shellfish farmers continually remove pests like slipper limpets and whelks from oyster and mussel beds.

The netted slug is a major pest on many crops, especially potatoes.

People have used sea shells as ornaments and for making jewelry for hundreds of years. Cameos are carved from large helmet shells and conchs, while mother-of-pearl comes from the lining of abalone shells. There is no harm in collecting empty shells for all these things, but people unfortunately kill large numbers of sea snails in order to sell their shells. To keep these animals from dying out, many countries now have laws preventing fishermen from collecting sea snails over a certain size.

There are other ways in which we can look after slugs and snails – by protecting their natural habitats and by keeping the ocean and other wild places clean and free from pollution.

7
Studying Slugs and Snails

A collection of limpet shells. When you are at the beach look for empty shells to start a collection of your own.

Studying Slugs and Snails

The best time to look for slugs and snails is on warm, damp evenings, after rain. If you take a flashlight you will almost certainly find them out feeding and perhaps even mating. Mark the spot carefully, and then go back and look for their slime trails the next day. Try following them to see where they lead.

You can learn much more about slugs and snails by keeping some inside a glass tank or "terrarium." The picture shows you how to set up your tank. Keep your terrarium in the shade and sprinkle the soil with water occasionally to keep the atmosphere moist. If you keep the lower part covered with a dark cloth or paper, this will encourage the animals to lay eggs against the glass, and you will be able to watch their development.

Do not forget to feed your pets. Try

offering them different kinds of green plants, as well as things such as dead leaves, chopped apple, potato, breadcrumbs, cheese or bits of raw meat. Be sure to clear away any uneaten food before it goes rotten. Keep a note of what foods they will and will not eat. You should have plenty of opportunity to watch and discover how your slugs or snails move, feed, breathe and perhaps even mate.

Keeping pond snails in a freshwater aquarium is a good way of learning more about them too. Sea slugs and snails are not so easy to keep at home. However, you can look for them on your next visit to the beach. Look into rock pools, search under stones and seaweed and peer into rock crevices when the tide is out.

zinc mesh lid for ventilation

turf

stones and broken flower pot for shelter

gravel for drainage

damp soil (10cm (4 in) deep) for laying eggs

moss

Glossary

Aestivation A long period spent sleeping underground or in a shady place, during a hot, dry spell.

Algae A group of simple plants (including seaweeds), many of which are microscopic and live in water.

Bivalves A group of mollusks whose bodies are enclosed in a hinged shell of two parts e.g. oysters, clams, mussels.

Carnivorous Flesh-eating.

Cilia Tiny, hair-like projections that beat rhythmically to produce movement or to create a current of water.

Fertilize To join the male sperm with the female egg, so that a new individual can grow from the fertilized egg.

Gastropods A group of mollusks that includes slugs and snails.

Gills Branched or comb-like structures used by many underwater animals for breathing.

Glands Parts of the body that produce a special substance, such as mucus, sweat or poison.

Habitat The place in which a plant or animal lives.

Herbivorous Plant-eating.

Hermaphrodite An animal that is both male and female.

Host An animal or plant in which a parasite lives.

Larvae (plural of larva) Young stages (hatching from the eggs) of many insects and underwater animals.

Lichens Crust-like, scaly or leafy plants, often found covering rocks, walls, tree trunks, etc.

Mantle The thin fold of skin covering the body of a mollusk from which the shell is produced.

Mollusks A large group of soft-bodied animals including gastropods, bivalves and animals like octopus and squid.

Mucus A slimy substance produced by many animals, including slugs and snails.

Operculum A horny plate on the foot of some snails that closes the shell opening when the snail retreats inside.

Parasitic Living and feeding on others.

Penis The male fertilizing organ.

Pesticides Poisonous chemicals used to kill pests.

Plankton Tiny animals and plants that float and drift near the surface of the sea.

Predators Animals that kill and eat other animals.

Prey Animals that are hunted and killed by predators.

Proboscis A snout-like projection, carrying the mouth.

Radula (pl. radulae) A tongue-like structure, bearing numerous horny teeth, found in most mollusks.

Scavenge To feed on dead animals or plants.

Sperm Male sex cells, used to fertilize a female's eggs.

Spicule A small hard dart-shaped structure.

Tropics Warm regions of the earth lying near the equator.

Finding Out More

The following book will help you to find out more about slugs and snails.

Animals that Live in Shells, by Morris Dean. Raintree, 1977.

The Encyclopedia of Marine Invertebrates, Jerry G. Walls, ed. T.F.H. Publications, 1982.

A First Look at Animals without Backbones, by Millicent Selsam and Joyce Hunt. Walker & Co., 1976.

Houses from the Sea, by Alice E. Goudey. Scribner, 1959.

Science-Hobby Book of Shell Collecting, by Mirian Gilbert. Lerner Publications, 1968.

Snails, by Syliva A. Johnson. Lerner Publications, 1982.

Snails of Land and Sea, by Hilda Simon. Vanguard, 1975.

Wonders of Snails and Slugs, by Morris K. Jacobson and David R. Franz. Dodd, 1980.

Index

Picture Acknowledgments

All photographs from Oxford Scientific Films by the following photographers: D. Allan 33 (left); T. Allen 41; G.I. Bernard *cover*, 9, 11 (top), 12, 13 (right), 14, 16, 18, 19, 20, 21 (right), 22, 27 (bottom), 28, 31, 32, 33 (right), 34, 38, 40; R. Blythe 37 (top); D. Clyne 30; J.A.L. Cooke 10, 11 (bottom), 15, 35 (left); Mantis Wildlife Films 37 (bottom); P. Parks *frontispiece*, 8, 24, 25; D.M. Shale 17, 29, 39; P.K. Sharpe 36; D. Thompson 27 (top); B.E. Watts 13 (left), 21 (left), 26; D. Wright 42. Artwork on page 43 by Jackie Harland.